NO-F[illegible]
MOCKTAILS

80 Easy and Delicious Non-Alcoholic Recipes for Every Occasion

ALICE JENNINGS

DJTS Publishing
info@djts-publishing.com

ISBN Paperback: 978-3-910634-21-3

Imprint: DJTS Publishing

TABLE OF CONTENTS

TABLE OF CONTENTS

Hello there,

Have you ever been at a party, wanting to enjoy the evening, yet not inclined towards alcoholic beverages? Have you ever thought about how wonderful it would be to have a selection of delicious, non-alcoholic drinks that match the mood, the food, and the company? It was a similar train of thought that inspired me to venture into the world of mocktails.

I've spent countless evenings experimenting in my kitchen, mixing and matching flavors until each mocktail recipe was as sophisticated, tantalizing, and satisfying as any cocktail could be. The result is a collection of 80 innovative, easy-to-make recipes that cater to every palate, every occasion, and every season.

But why mocktails? Why dedicate an entire book to alcohol-free beverages?

The answer lies in the magic that mocktails bring to the table. They allow everyone, regardless of their preference for alcohol, to partake in the joy of a beautifully crafted drink. They offer a creative outlet for the hosts, a delightful surprise for the guests, and a healthier choice for everyone. Most importantly, they affirm that the essence of a good party is not in the alcohol served. Still, in the companionship shared, the conversations sparked, and the memories created.

The beauty of this book lies in its simplicity. Every recipe this book shares has been crafted with the beginner in mind. Each is a story of flavor and finesse, made accessible to everyone, regardless of their experience behind the bar. Remember the first time you created a meal from scratch? The joy of seeing simple ingredients transform into something deliciously complex? That's the feeling you'll relive each time you craft a mocktail from this book.

So, are you ready to transform your social gatherings with these flavorful, non-alcoholic delights? Are you prepared to become the host with the most exciting, inclusive, and memorable drink menu? Join me in this journey through "No-Fuss "as we explore the boundless possibilities of alcohol-free mixology. Let's raise a glass to healthier choices, inclusive gatherings, and unforgettable moments. Cheers to the joy of mocktails!

Feel free to contact me if you have any questions or suggestions.
You can reach me at: authors@djts-publishing.com

VIRGIN PINA COLADA

PREPARATION TIME
10 Min

COOL-DOWN TIME
0 Min

SERVINGS
1

Ingredients

- 1 cup (240 mL) pineapple juice
- 1/2 cup (120 mL) coconut milk
- 1 tablespoon (15 mL) fresh lime juice
- 1/2 cup (120 mL) crushed ice
- Pineapple slice for garnish
- Maraschino cherry, for garnish

Directions

1. Add pineapple juice, coconut milk, fresh lime juice, and crushed ice into a blender.
2. Blend until the mixture turns smooth and frothy.
3. Pour your homemade Virgin Pina Colada into a chilled hurricane glass.
4. Embellish your mocktail with a slice of pineapple and a Maraschino cherry before serving.

GINGER BEER SHANDY

PREPARATION TIME
5 Min

COOL-DOWN TIME
0 Min

SERVINGS
1

Ingredients

- 1 cup (240 mL) ginger beer
- 1/2 cup (120 mL) lemonade
- 1/2 cup (120 mL) club soda
- Lemon wheel, for garnish

Directions

1. Fill a pint glass halfway with ice. Pour ginger beer into the glass.
2. Add in lemonade, and top it off with club soda. Stir gently to mix the ingredients well.
3. Place a lemon wheel on the rim of the glass for garnish, and serve your Ginger Beer Shandy immediately.

GRAPEFRUIT AND ROSEMARY MOCKTAIL

PREPARATION TIME
10 Min

COOL-DOWN TIME
0 Min

SERVINGS
1

Ingredients

- 1/2 cup (120 mL) fresh grapefruit juice
- 1/4 cup (60 mL) rosemary simple syrup (boil 2 cup water and sugar with 2 sprigs of rosemary)
- 1/2 cup (120 mL) club soda
- Ice cubes
- Rosemary sprig and grapefruit wedge for garnish

Directions

1. Fill a rocks glass with ice cubes. Pour the grapefruit juice and rosemary simple syrup over the ice.
2. Top off with club soda and give a gentle stir to combine.
3. Garnish the mocktail with a sprig of rosemary and a wedge of grapefruit, then serve.

ROSE FIZZ

PREPARATION TIME
5 Min

COOL-DOWN TIME
0 Min

SERVINGS
1

Ingredients

- 1 egg white
- 1 teaspoon powdered sugar
- 1/2 ounce (15 mL) fresh lemon juice
- Fentimans Rose Lemonade to top

Directions

1. Combine the egg white, powdered sugar, and fresh lemon juice in a cocktail shaker. Shake well without ice. This is known as a dry shake.
2. Add ice into the shaker and shake vigorously until the mixture has an almost foamy texture.
3. Strain the mixture into a chilled glass. Top with Fentimans Rose Lemonade, then serve immediately.

HONEY LEMONADE

PREPARATION TIME
5 Min

COOL-DOWN TIME
0 Min

SERVINGS
1

Ingredients

- 1/2 cup (120 mL) fresh lemon juice
- 2 tablespoons (30 mL) honey
- 1 cup (240 mL) water
- Ice cubes
- Lemon slice, for garnish

Directions

1. Combine the lemon juice and honey in a glass until the honey is completely dissolved.
2. Add water to the glass and mix thoroughly. Fill the glass with shards of ice.
3. Before serving, add a lemon segment as a garnish.

BLUEBERRY MOJITO MOCKTAIL

PREPARATION TIME
10 Min

COOL-DOWN TIME
0 Min

SERVINGS
1

Ingredients

- 1/2 cup (70 g) fresh blueberries
- 10 fresh mint leaves
- 2 teaspoons (10 mL) sugar
- Juice of 1 lime
- 1/2 cup (120 mL) club soda
- Ice cubes
- Mint sprig and a lime wheel for garnish

Directions

1. In a glass, muddle the blueberries, mint leaves, and sugar until the sugar dissolves and the blueberries are crushed.
2. Add the lime juice to the glass. Fill the glass with ice cubes.
3. Top off with club soda and give a gentle stir to combine.
4. Add a mint leaf and a lime wheel to the top before serving.

NON-ALCOHOLIC SANGRIA

PREPARATION TIME
15 Min

COOL-DOWN TIME
120 Min

SERVINGS
4

Ingredients

- 1 apple, chopped
- 1 orange, sliced
- 1 lemon, sliced
- 1 cup (240 mL) orange juice
- 2 cups (480 mL) cranberry juice
- 1 cup (240 mL) pineapple juice
- 2 cups (480 mL) sparkling water

Directions

1. In a large pitcher, combine the chopped apple and the slices of orange and lemon.
2. Add the orange, cranberry, and pineapple juice to the pitcher and stir to combine.
3. Stir gently, then refrigerate for at least 120 Minutes to let the flavors meld together.
4. Add the sparkling water to the pitcher before serving and stir gently. Fill flutes with ice and pour sangria on top.

WATERMELON LEMONADE

PREPARATION TIME
15 Min

COOL-DOWN TIME
60 Min

SERVINGS
4

Ingredients

- 4 cups (950 mL) cubed watermelon
- 1 cup (240 mL) fresh lemon juice
- 1/2 cup (100 g) sugar
- 4 cups (950 mL) cold water
- Ice cubes
- Lemon slices and watermelon wedges for garnish

Directions

1. Blend the watermelon in a blender until it is smooth. Use a fine-mesh sieve to pour the watermelon juice into a big pitcher.
2. Put the sugar and lemon juice in the pitcher & stir until the sugar is dissolved.
3. Mix in the cold water by stirring. Cool in the freezer for about 60 minutes. Pour the lemonade over the ice cubes into the cups.
4. Before serving, add a slice of lemon and a piece of watermelon.

VIRGIN STRAWBERRY DAIQUIRI

PREPARATION TIME
10 Min

COOL-DOWN TIME
0

SERVINGS
1

Ingredients

- 1 cup (150 g) fresh strawberries
- 1 tablespoon (15 mL) fresh lime juice
- 2 tablespoons (25 g) sugar
- 1/2 cup (120 mL) ice cubes
- Strawberry and lime wheel for garnish

Directions

1. Combine the strawberries, lime juice, sugar, and ice cubes in a blender.
2. Blend until smooth and frothy. Pour into a chilled glass. Garnish with a strawberry and a lime wheel before serving.

ORANGE SUNRISE FIZZ

PREPARATION TIME
5 Min

COOL-DOWN TIME
0 Min

SERVINGS
1

Ingredients

- 1 cup (240 mL) orange juice
- 1/2 cup (120 mL) club soda
- 1 tablespoon (15 mL) grenadine
- Ice cubes
- Orange wheel, for garnish

Directions

1. Fill a glass with ice cubes. Pour the orange juice into the glass.
2. Top off with club soda. Slowly pour the grenadine into the glass. It will sink to the bottom, creating a beautiful sunrise effect.
3. Garnish with an orange wheel before serving.

APPLE GINGER SPARKLER

PREPARATION TIME
5 Min

COOL-DOWN TIME
0 Min

SERVINGS
1

Ingredients

- 1 cup (240 mL) apple cider (non-alcoholic)
- 1/2 cup (120 mL) ginger beer
- 1/2 cup (120 mL) club soda
- Apple slices and cinnamon stick for garnish

Directions

1. Fill ice in a tall goblet. The apple cider is poured into the glass.
2. Add ginger beer before topping with club seltzer. Stir with care to combine.
3. Before serving, garnish with apple slices and a cinnamon stick.

BERRY GOOD LEMONADE

PREPARATION TIME
10 Min

COOL-DOWN TIME
60 Min

SERVINGS
4

Ingredients

- 1 cup (240 mL) fresh lemon juice
- 3/4 cup (150 g) sugar
- 4 cups (950 mL) cold water
- 1 cup (150 g) mixed berries (like strawberries, raspberries, and blueberries)
- Ice cubes
- Lemon wheels and mixed berries for garnish

Directions

1. In a pitcher, combine the lime juice & sugar. Stir until the sugar is fully dissolved.
2. Add the cold water and mixed berries to the pitcher and stir to combine.
3. Refrigerate for at least 60 minutes to cool and let the flavors infuse.
4. Put the ice cubes in the glasses and pour the lemonade over the ice.
5. Garnish with a lemon wheel and some mixed berries before serving.

PEACHY ICED GREEN TEA

PREPARATION TIME
15 Min

COOL-DOWN TIME
60 Min

SERVINGS
4

Ingredients

- 4 green tea bags
- 4 cups (950 mL) boiling water
- 1 peach, sliced
- 2 tablespoons (30 mL) honey
- Ice cubes
- Peach slices and mint sprigs for garnish

Directions

1. Put the tea bags in a big pitcher that can handle the heat. Put the hot water over the tea bags and let them sit for 5 mins.
2. Take the tea bags out of the bowl and add the peach slices and honey.
3. Stir until all of the honey is gone. Please put it in the freezer for at least 60 minutes to cool it down and let the flavors mix.
4. Fill cups with ice cubes, then pour the iced tea over the ice.
5. Before serving, add a slice of peach and a sprig of mint to the top.

SPARKLING RASPBERRY LIME MOCKTAIL

PREPARATION TIME
5 Min

COOL-DOWN TIME
0 Min

SERVINGS
1

Ingredients

- 1/2 cup (60 g) fresh raspberries
- 1 tablespoon (15 mL) fresh lime juice
- 1 teaspoon (5 g) sugar
- 1 cup (240 mL) sparkling water
- Ice cubes
- Lime wheel and fresh raspberries for garnish

Directions

1. Mix the raspberries, lime juice, and sugar in a glass until the sugar has melted and the raspberries are completely broken.
2. Put ice cubes in the glass. Pour sparkling water on top, and stir gently to mix.
3. Before serving, top with a lime wheel and a few fresh strawberries.

CITRUS FIZZ

PREPARATION TIME
5 Min

COOL-DOWN TIME
0 Min

SERVINGS
1

Ingredients

- 1/4 cup (60 mL) fresh orange juice
- 1/4 cup (60 mL) fresh lime juice
- 1/4 cup (60 mL) fresh lime juice
- 2 tablespoons (30 mL) simple syrup
- Club soda, to top
- Lemon, lime, and orange slices for garnish

Directions

1. Fill a highball glass with ice. Add the orange juice, lemon juice, lime juice, and simple syrup into the glass.
2. Top with club soda. Stir gently to mix.
3. Garnish with lemon, lime, and orange slices, then serve immediately.

CRANBERRY MOCKTAIL

PREPARATION TIME
5 Min

COOL-DOWN TIME
0 Min

SERVINGS
1

Ingredients

- 1 cup (240 mL) cranberry juice
- 1/2 cup (120 mL) sparkling water
- 1 tablespoon (15 mL) fresh lime juice
- Ice cubes
- Lime wheel and cranberries for garnish

Directions

1. Fill a tall glass with ice cubes. Pour the cranberry juice into the glass.
2. Add the sparkling water and lime juice, then stir gently to combine. Add a lime wheel and a few fruits to the top of the drink before serving.

STRAWBERRY BASIL SODA

PREPARATION TIME
10 Min

COOL-DOWN TIME
60 Min

SERVINGS
4

Ingredients

- 1 cup (150 g) fresh strawberries, hulled and halved
- 10 fresh basil leaves
- 2 tablespoons (25 g) sugar
- 4 cups (950 mL) of club soda
- Ice cubes
- Strawberry slices and basil leaves for garnish

Directions

1. In a large pitcher, muddle the strawberries, basil leaves, and sugar until the sugar dissolves and the strawberries are crushed.
2. Add the club soda to the pitcher & stir gently to combine. Freeze for at least 60 minutes to let the flavors infuse.
3. The soda should be served in glasses filled with ice. Serve with a basil leaf and strawberry slice for garnish.

BLACKBERRY LEMON MOCKTAIL

PREPARATION TIME
10 Min

COOL-DOWN TIME
0 Min

SERVINGS
1

Ingredients

- 1/2 cup (60 g) fresh blackberries
- 1 tablespoon (15 mL) fresh lemon juice
- 1 teaspoon (5 g) sugar
- 1 cup (240 mL) sparkling water
- Ice cubes
- Lemon wheel and fresh blackberries for garnish

Directions

1. In a glass, muddle the blackberries, lemon juice, and sugar until the sugar dissolves and the blackberries are crushed.
2. Fill the glass with ice cubes.
3. Top off with sparkling water and stir generously to combine.
4. Before serving, garnish with lime zest and a few fresh blackberries.

VIRGIN MOJITO

PREPARATION TIME
10 Min

COOL-DOWN TIME
0 Min

SERVINGS
1

Ingredients

- 10 fresh mint leaves
- 1 tablespoon (15 mL) fresh lime juice
- 2 teaspoons (10 g) sugar
- 1/2 cup (120 mL) club soda
- Ice cubes
- Lime wheel and fresh mint sprig for garnishing

Directions

1. 10 fresh mint leaves
2. 1 tablespoon (15 mL) fresh lime juice
3. 2 teaspoons (10 g) sugar
4. 1/2 cup (120 mL) club soda
5. Ice cubes
6. Lime wheel and fresh mint sprig for garnishing

MAGIC APPLE

PREPARATION TIME
10 Min

COOL-DOWN TIME
0 Min

SERVINGS
1

Ingredients

- 1/2 green apple
- 1 tablespoon (15 mL) fresh lime juice
- 1/2 cup (120 mL) apple juice
- 1/2 cup (120 mL) sparkling water
- 1 teaspoon (5 mL) honey, optional
- Mint leaves, for garnish
- Apple slice, for garnish

Directions

1. Juice the green apple or blend and strain to get the juice.
2. In a glass, combine the green apple juice, lime juice, apple juice, and honey if desired.
3. Stir well until the honey is dissolved. Top up with sparkling water.
4. Garnish with apple slices and mint leaves. Serve immediately and enjoy the magic of the apple!

CUCUMBER LIME MOCKTAIL

PREPARATION TIME
10 Min

COOL-DOWN TIME
0 Min

SERVINGS
1

Ingredients

- 1/4 cup (60 g) chopped cucumber
- 1 tablespoon (15 mL) fresh lime juice
- 1 teaspoon (5 g) sugar
- 1 cup (240 mL) sparkling water
- Ice cubes
- Lime wheel and cucumber slice for garnish

Directions

1. Muddle the cucumber, lime juice, and sugar in a glass until the sugar is melted and the cucumber is broken.
2. Fill the glass halfway with ice cubes. Top with sparkling water and gently whisk to blend.
3. Before serving, garnish with a lime wheel and a slice of cucumber.

POMEGRANATE SPRITZER

PREPARATION TIME
5 Min

COOL-DOWN TIME
0 Min

SERVINGS
1

Ingredients

- 1 cup (240 mL) pomegranate juice
- 1/2 cup (120 mL) sparkling water
- Ice cubes
- Pomegranate seeds and orange wheel for garnish

Directions

1. Fill a tall glass with ice cubes. Pour the pomegranate juice into the glass.
2. Top off with sparkling water and stir generously to combine. Garnish with a sprinkle of pomegranate seeds and an orange wheel before serving.

WATERMELON COOLER

PREPARATION TIME
10 Min

COOL-DOWN TIME
0 Min

SERVINGS
2

Ingredients

- 2 cups (300 g) cubed watermelon
- 1 cup (240 mL) coconut water
- Juice of 1 lime
- 1 cup (240 mL) ice cubes
- Watermelon slice and mint sprig for garnish

Directions

1. Combine the watermelon cubes, coconut water, and lime juice in a blender.
2. Blend until smooth. Add the ice cubes and pulse a few times to crush the ice. Before serving, pour them into glasses and top with slices of watermelon and a sprig of mint.

CHERRY LIMEADE

PREPARATION TIME
10 Min

COOL-DOWN TIME
60 Min

SERVINGS
4

Ingredients

- 1 cup (240 mL) fresh lime juice
- 3/4 cup (150 g) sugar
- 4 cups (950 mL) cold water
- 1 cup (155 g) pitted cherries
- Ice cubes
- Lime wheels and cherries for garnish

Directions

1. In a pitcher, combine the lime juice and sugar. Stir until the sugar is fully dissolved.
2. Add the cold water and cherries to the pitcher and stir to combine.
3. Refrigerate for at least 60 minutes to cool and let the flavors infuse. Pour limeade into ice-filled cups.
4. Serve with lime and cherry garnishes.

PEACH LEMONADE

PREPARATION TIME
10 Min

COOL-DOWN TIME
60 Min

SERVINGS
4

Ingredients

- 4 peaches, pitted and quartered
- 1 cup (240 mL) fresh lemon juice
- 3/4 cup (150 g) sugar
- 4 cups (950 mL) cold water
- Ice cubes
- Lemon wheels and peach slices for garnish

Directions

1. In a blender, combine the peaches, lemon juice, and sugar. Blend until smooth.
2. Pour the blending through a sieve into a large pitcher, discarding the peach pulp.
3. Add the cold water to the pitcher and stir to combine.
4. Refrigerate for at least 60 minutes to cool. Fill glasses with ice cubes & pour the lemonade over the ice.
5. Garnish with a lemon wheel and a peach slice before serving.

MANGO MOCKTAIL

PREPARATION TIME
10 Min

COOL-DOWN TIME
0 Min

SERVINGS
2

Ingredients

- 2 ripe mangoes, peeled and pitted
- 1 cup (240 mL) orange juice
- 1 cup (240 mL) sparkling water
- Ice cubes
- Orange wheel and fresh mint sprig for garnish

Directions

1. In a blender, combine the mangoes and orange juice.
2. Blend until smooth. Fill glasses with ice cubes.
3. Pour the mango mixture into the glasses, then top off with sparkling water.
4. Stir gently to combine, then garnish with an orange wheel and a sprig of fresh mint before serving.

BLUEBERRY LEMON MOCKTAIL

PREPARATION TIME
10 Min

COOL-DOWN TIME
0 Min

SERVINGS
1

Ingredients

- 1/2 cup (50 g) fresh blueberries
- 1 tablespoon (15 mL) fresh lemon juice
- 1 teaspoon (5 g) sugar
- 1 cup (240 mL) sparkling water
- Ice cubes
- Lemon wheel and fresh blueberries for garnish

Directions

1. In a glass, muddle the blueberries, lemon juice, and sugar till the sugar is dissolved and the blueberries are crushed.
2. Ice cubes should be put in the glass. Finish off with sparkling water and stir gently to combine.
3. Before serving, garnish with a lemon wheel and some fresh blueberries.

VIRGIN MARY

PREPARATION TIME
5 Min

COOL-DOWN TIME
0 Min

SERVINGS
1

Ingredients

- 1 cup (240 mL) tomato juice
- 1 tablespoon (15 mL) fresh lemon juice
- 1/4 teaspoon (1.25 mL) Worcestershire sauce
- 1/4 teaspoon (1.25 mL) hot sauce
- Celery salt and black pepper, to taste
- Ice cubes
- Celery stalk and lemon wheel for garnish

Directions

1. Combine the tomato juice, lemon juice, Worcestershire sauce, and hot sauce in a tall glass.
2. Season with celery salt and black pepper to taste.
3. Fill the glass with ice cubes, and then stir to combine.
4. Garnish with a celery stalk & a lemon wheel before serving.

APPLE GINGER MOCKTAIL

PREPARATION TIME
5 Min

COOL-DOWN TIME
0 Min

SERVINGS
1

Ingredients

- 1 cup (240 mL) apple juice
- 1/2 teaspoon (2.5 mL) fresh ginger, grated
- 1/2 cup (120 mL) ginger ale
- Ice cubes
- Apple slice and fresh mint sprig for garnish

Directions

1. In a tall glass, combine the apple juice and grated ginger.
2. Fill the glass with ice cubes. Top off with ginger ale and stir gently to combine.
3. Before serving, garnish with an apple slice and a sprig of fresh mint.

TROPICAL MOCKTAIL

PREPARATION TIME
10 Min

COOL-DOWN TIME
0 Min

SERVINGS
2

Ingredients

- 1 cup (240 mL) pineapple juice
- 1 cup (240 mL) coconut water
- 1 cup (240 mL) orange juice
- 1 cup (240 mL) ice cubes
- Pineapple slice, orange wheel, and maraschino cherry for garnish

Directions

1. Combine the pineapple juice, coconut water, and orange juice in a blender.
2. Add the ice cubes and pulse a few times to crush the ice.
3. Place in glasses and garnish with a slice of pineapple, an orange wheel, and a maraschino cherry before serving.

STRAWBERRY BASIL MOCKTAIL

PREPARATION TIME
10 Min

COOL-DOWN TIME
0 Min

SERVINGS
1

Ingredients

- 1/2 cup (75 g) fresh strawberries
- 2 fresh basil leaves
- 1 tablespoon (15 mL) fresh lime juice
- 1 teaspoon (5 g) sugar
- 1 cup (240 mL) sparkling water
- Ice cubes
- Strawberry slice and fresh basil leaf for garnish

Directions

1. In a glass, muddle the strawberries, basil leaves, lime juice & sugar until the sugar is dissolved and the strawberries are crushed.
2. Fill the glass with ice cubes. Top off with sparkling water & stir gently to combine.
3. Garnish with a strawberry slice and a fresh basil leaf before serving.

RASPBERRY MINT MOCKTAIL

PREPARATION TIME
10 Min

COOL-DOWN TIME
0 Min

SERVINGS
1

Ingredients

- 1/2 cup (60 g) fresh raspberries
- 10 fresh mint leaves
- 1 tablespoon (15 mL) fresh lime juice
- 1 teaspoon (5 g) sugar
- 1 cup (240 mL) sparkling water
- Ice cubes
- Raspberry and mint sprig for garnish

Directions

1. Raspberries, mint leaves, lime juice, and sugar are muddled in a glass until the sugar is dissolved and the raspberries are pulverized.
2. Fill the glass with shards of ice. Add carbonated water and stir gently to incorporate.
3. Before serving, garnish with a fresh raspberry and a mint sprig.

PEAR GINGER MOCKTAIL

PREPARATION TIME
5 Min

COOL-DOWN TIME
0 Min

SERVINGS
1

Ingredients

- 1 cup (240 mL) pear juice
- 1/2 teaspoon (2.5 mL) fresh ginger, grated
- 1/2 cup (120 mL) ginger ale
- Ice cubes
- Pear slice and fresh mint sprig for garnish

Directions

1. In a tall glass, combine the pear juice and grated ginger.
2. Fill the glass with ice cubes. Top off with ginger ale and stir gently to combine.
3. Garnish with a pear slice and a sprig of fresh mint before serving.

KIWI COOLER

PREPARATION TIME
10 Min

COOL-DOWN TIME
0 Min

SERVINGS
2

Ingredients

- 3 ripe kiwis, peeled
- 1 cup (240 mL) apple juice
- 1 cup (240 mL) sparkling water
- Ice cubes
- Kiwi slice and apple slice for garnish

Directions

1. In a blender, combine the kiwis and apple juice. Blend until smooth.
2. Fill glasses with ice cubes. Pour the kiwi mixture into the glasses, then top off with sparkling water.
3. Stir gently to combine, then garnish with a kiwi and apple slices before serving.

HONEYDEW LIME MOCKTAIL

PREPARATION TIME
10 Min

COOL-DOWN TIME
0 Min

SERVINGS
2

Ingredients

- 2 cups (320 g) honeydew melon, cubed
- 1 cup (240 mL) lime juice
- 1 cup (240 mL) sparkling water
- Ice cubes
- Lime wheel and melon ball for garnish

Directions

1. In a blender, combine the honeydew melon and lime juice.
2. Blend until smooth. Fill glasses with ice cubes.
3. Pour the melon mixture into the glasses, then top off with sparkling water.
4. Stir gently to combine, then garnish with a lime wheel and a melon ball before serving.

WATERMELON MINT MOCKTAIL

PREPARATION TIME
10 Min

COOL-DOWN TIME
0 Min

SERVINGS
1

Ingredients

- 2 cups (320 g) watermelon, cubed
- 10 fresh mint leaves
- 1 cup (240 mL) sparkling water
- Ice cubes
- Watermelon slice and mint sprig for garnish

Directions

1. In a blender, combine the watermelon and mint leaves.
2. Blend until smooth.
3. Fill glasses with ice cubes.
4. Pour the watermelon mixture into the glasses, then top off with sparkling water.
5. Stir gently to combine, then garnish with a watermelon slice and a sprig of fresh mint before serving.

BERRY BURLESQUE

PREPARATION TIME
5 Min

COOL-DOWN TIME
0 Min

SERVINGS
1

Ingredients

- 1/2 cup (120 mL) mixed berry juice (raspberries, blackberries, blueberries)
- 1/4 cup (60 mL) lemon juice
- 1/4 cup (60 mL) simple syrup
- Soda water, to top
- Mixed berries and lemon slices for garnish

Directions

1. Fill a highball glass with ice.
2. Add mixed berry, lemon, and simple syrup into the glass.
3. Top with soda water. Stir gently to mix.
4. Garnish with mixed berries and lemon slices, then serve immediately.

BLACKBERRY SAGE MOCKTAIL

PREPARATION TIME
10 Min

COOL-DOWN TIME
0 Min

SERVINGS
1

Ingredients

- 1/2 cup (70 g) fresh blackberries
- 2 fresh sage leaves
- 1 tablespoon (15 mL) fresh lemon juice
- 1 teaspoon (5 g) sugar
- 1 cup (240 mL) sparkling water
- Ice cubes
- Blackberry and sage leaf for garnish

Directions

1. In a glass, muddle the blackberries, sage leaves, lemon juice & sugar until the sugar is dissolved and the blackberries are crushed.
2. Fill the glass with ice cubes.
3. Top off with sparkling water and stir generously to combine.
4. Garnish with a fresh blackberry and a sage leaf before serving.

PINEAPPLE COCONUT MOCKTAIL

PREPARATION TIME
10 Min

COOL-DOWN TIME
0 Min

SERVINGS
2

Ingredients

- 1 cup (240 mL) pineapple juice
- 1 cup (240 mL) coconut water
- 1 cup (240 mL) ice cubes
- Pineapple slice and maraschino cherry for garnish

Directions

1. In a blender, combine the pineapple juice and coconut water. Add the ice cubes and pulse a few times to crush the ice.
2. Pour into glasses & garnish with a pineapple slice and a maraschino cherry before serving.

VANTAGE POINT

PREPARATION TIME
5 Min

COOL-DOWN TIME
0 Min

SERVINGS
1

Ingredients

- 1/2 cup (120 mL) ginger ale
- 1/2 cup (120 mL) tonic water
- 1 tablespoon (15 mL) lime juice
- 1 tablespoon (15 mL) cranberry juice
- Lime wheel, for garnish

Directions

1. Fill a highball glass with ice.
2. Add the ginger ale, tonic water, lime juice, and cranberry juice into the glass.
3. Stir gently to mix. Garnish with a lime wheel, then serve immediately.

SEEDLIP SPICE & TONIC

PREPARATION TIME
5 Min

COOL-DOWN TIME
0 Min

SERVINGS
1

Ingredients

- 2 ounces (60 mL) Seedlip Spice 94
- 4 ounces (120 mL) premium tonic water
- Lime wedge for garnish
- Ice cubes

Directions

1. Fill a highball glass with ice cubes.
2. Pour the Seedlip Spice 94 over the ice.
3. Top with premium tonic water. Stir gently to combine.
4. Garnish with a lime wedge and serve right away.

STRAWBERRY LEMONADE MOCKTAIL

PREPARATION TIME
10 Min

COOL-DOWN TIME
60 Min

SERVINGS
2

Ingredients

- 1 cup (150 g) fresh strawberries
- 1 cup (240 mL) fresh lemon juice
- 3/4 cup (150 g) sugar
- 4 cups (950 mL) cold water
- Ice cubes
- Lemon wheels and strawberry slices for garnish

Directions

1. In a blender, combine the strawberries, lemon juice, and sugar.
2. Blend until smooth.
3. Pour the blending through a sieve into a large pitcher, discarding the strawberry pulp.
4. Add the cold water to the pitcher and stir to combine.
5. Refrigerate for at least 60 minutes to cool.
6. Fill glasses with ice cubes & the lemonade over the ice.
7. Serve with a strawberry slice and a lemon wheel for garnish.

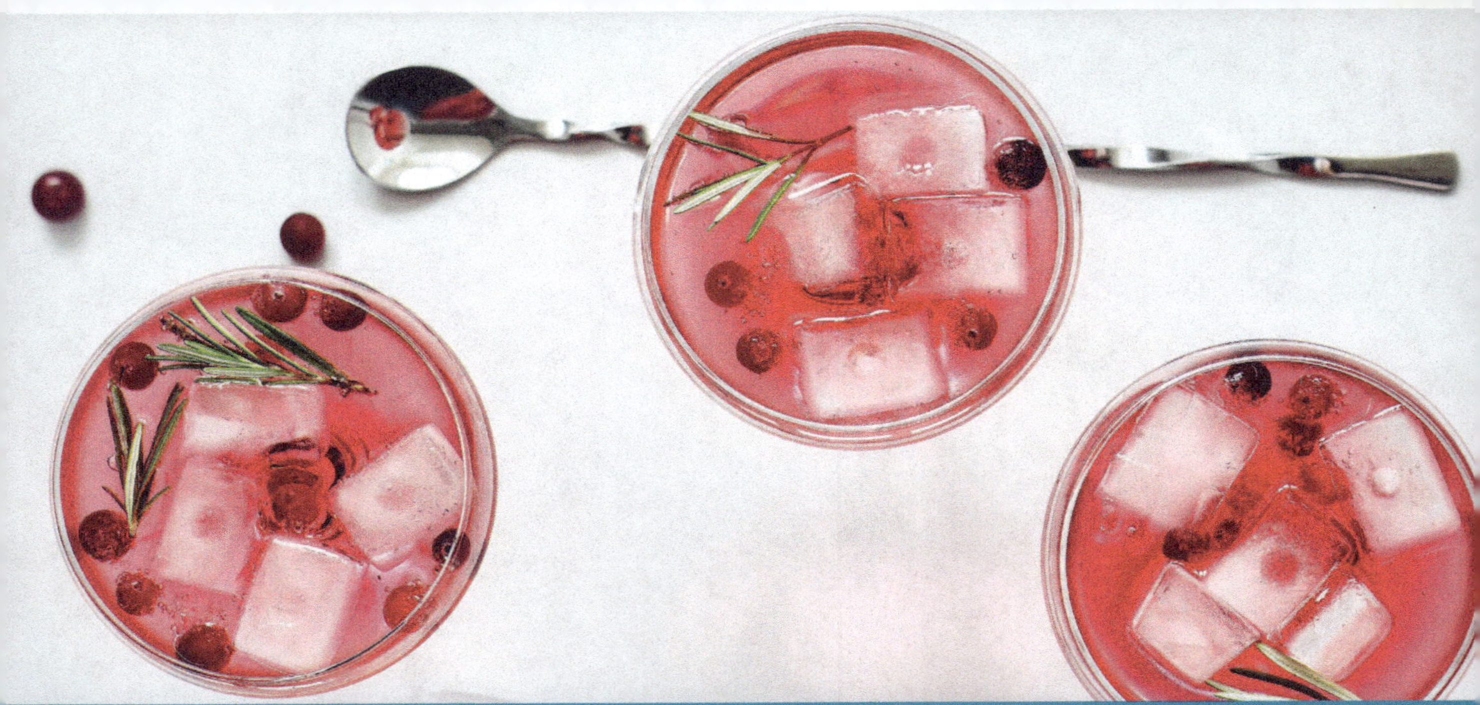

CRANBERRY MOCKTAIL

PREPARATION TIME
5 Min

COOL-DOWN TIME
0 Min

SERVINGS
1

Ingredients

- 1 cup (240 mL) cranberry juice
- 1 tablespoon (15 mL) fresh lime juice
- 1 cup (240 mL) soda water
- Ice cubes
- Lime wheel and fresh cranberries for garnish

Directions

1. In a tall glass, combine the cranberry juice and lime juice.
2. Fill the glass with ice cubes. Top off with soda water and stir generously to combine.
3. Add a lime wheel and a few fresh cherries to the top of the drink before serving.

ORANGE GINGER MOCKTAIL

PREPARATION TIME
5 Min

COOL-DOWN TIME
0 Min

SERVINGS
1

Ingredients

- 1 cup (240 mL) orange juice
- 1/2 teaspoon (2.5 mL) fresh ginger, grated
- 1 cup (240 mL) ginger ale
- Ice cubes
- Orange wheel and fresh mint sprig for garnish

Directions

1. In a tall glass, combine the orange juice and grated ginger.
2. Fill the glass with ice cubes. Top off with ginger ale and stir gently to combine.
3. Garnish with an orange wheel and a sprig of fresh mint before serving.

POMEGRANATE MOCKTAIL

PREPARATION TIME
5 Min

COOL-DOWN TIME
0 Min

SERVINGS
1

Ingredients

- 1 cup (240 mL) pomegranate juice
- 1 tablespoon (15 mL) fresh lime juice
- 1 cup (240 mL) soda water
- Ice cubes
- Lime wheel and pomegranate seeds for garnish

Directions

1. In a tall glass, combine the pomegranate juice and lime juice.
2. Fill the glass with ice cubes.
3. Top off with soda water and stir generously to combine.
4. Add a lime wheel and pomegranate seeds before serving.

PEACH ICED TEA MOCKTAIL

PREPARATION TIME
10 Min

COOL-DOWN TIME
60 Min

SERVINGS
2

Ingredients

- 2 tea bags
- 2 cups (480 mL) boiling water
- 1 cup (240 mL) peach juice
- Ice cubes
- Fresh peach slices and fresh mint sprigs for garnish

Directions

1. Steep the tea bags in the water that is boiling for 5 minutes.
2. After the tea has reached room temperature, remove and discard the tea bags.
3. Combine the peach juice and cooled tea in a big pitcher.
4. Please put it in the refrigerator for 60 minutes to chill down.
5. Put ice cubes in cups and pour the iced tea in.
6. Before serving, top each glass with a piece of sliced peach and a sprig of fresh mint.

LAVENDER LEMONADE MOCKTAIL

PREPARATION TIME
10 Min

COOL-DOWN TIME
60 Min

SERVINGS
2

Ingredients

- 1 cup (240 mL) fresh lemon juice
- 3/4 cup (150 g) sugar
- 1 tablespoon (15 mL) dried lavender
- 4 cups (950 mL) cold water
- Ice cubes
- Lemon wheels and fresh lavender sprigs for garnish

Directions

1. Combine the lemon juice, sugar, and dried lavender in a large pitcher.
2. Stir until the sugar is dissolved. Add the cold water and stir to combine.
3. Refrigerate for at least 60 minutes to cool and infuse the lavender flavor.
4. Pour the lemonade over the ice cubes into the cups.
5. Before serving, add a slice of lemon and a sprig of fresh lavender.

PINA SERRANO MARGARITA

PREPARATION TIME
5 Min

COOL-DOWN TIME
0 Min

SERVINGS
1

Ingredients

- 1 ounce (30 mL) Optimist Smokey Non-Alc Tequila
- 2-4 slices of serrano pepper
- 2 ounces (60 mL) pineapple juice
- 1/2 ounce (15 mL) lime juice
- 1/2 ounce (15 mL) simple syrup

Directions

1. In a shaker, gently muddle the serrano pepper slices.
2. Add the Optimist Smokey Non-Alc Tequila, pineapple juice, lime juice, & simple syrup to the shaker.
3. Fill the shaker with ice. Shake vigorously until chilled.
4. Strain the blending into a rocks glass filled with fresh ice. Garnish with additional serrano coins for extra heat.
5. Serve immediately and enjoy the Pina Serrano Margarita!

MANGO GINGER MOCKTAIL

PREPARATION TIME
10 Min

COOL-DOWN TIME
2 Min

SERVINGS
2

Ingredients

- 2 ripe mangoes, peeled and chopped
- 1/2 teaspoon (2.5 mL) fresh ginger, grated
- 1 cup (240 mL) ginger ale
- Ice cubes
- Mango slice and fresh mint sprig for garnish

Directions

1. In a blender, combine the mangoes and grated ginger.
2. Blend until smooth. Fill glasses with ice cubes.
3. Pour the mango mixture into the glasses, then top off with ginger ale.
4. Stir gently to combine, then garnish with a mango slice and a sprig of fresh mint before serving.

APPLE CIDER MOCKTAIL

PREPARATION TIME
5 Min

COOL-DOWN TIME
0 Min

SERVINGS
2

Ingredients

- 2 cups (480 mL) apple cider (non-alcoholic)
- 1/2 teaspoon (2.5 mL) cinnamon
- 1/2 teaspoon (2.5 mL) nutmeg
- 1 cup (240 mL) soda water
- Ice cubes
- Apple slice and cinnamon stick for garnish

Directions

1. Combine the apple cider, cinnamon, and nutmeg in a large pitcher.
2. Stir until well combined. Fill glasses with ice cubes.
3. Pour the cider mixture into the glasses, then top off with soda water.
4. Stir gently to combine, then garnish with an apple slice and a cinnamon stick before serving.

TROPICAL PARADISE

PREPARATION TIME
5 Min

COOL-DOWN TIME
0 Min

SERVINGS
1

Ingredients

- 1/2 cup (120 mL) pineapple juice
- 1/2 cup (120 mL) orange juice
- 1/2 cup (120 mL) coconut milk
- Ice cubes
- Pineapple slice for garnish

Directions

1. Combine pineapple juice, orange juice & coconut milk in a cocktail shaker.
2. Shake well to combine. Strain the blending into a glass filled with ice cubes.
3. Garnish with a pineapple slice and serve.

CARAMEL APPLE MOCKTAIL

PREPARATION TIME
15 Min

COOL-DOWN TIME
10 Min

SERVINGS
2

Ingredients

- 1 cup (240 mL) apple juice
- 2 tablespoons (30 mL) caramel sauce
- 1/2 cup (120 mL) sparkling water
- Apple slices, for garnish

Directions

1. Pour the apple juice into a small non-stick saucepan and simmer over medium heat.
2. Add the caramel sauce and stir until fully incorporated. Allow it to cool for 10 minutes.
3. Pour the caramel apple mixture into two glasses.
4. Top each glass with sparkling water and garnish with apple slices before serving.

HOT CHOCOLATE MOCKTAIL

PREPARATION TIME
15 Min

COOL-DOWN TIME
5 Min

SERVINGS
2

Ingredients

- 2 cups (480 mL) milk
- 2 tablespoons (30 mL) unsweetened cocoa powder
- 2 tablespoons (30 mL) sugar
- Whipped cream and chocolate shavings for garnish

Directions

1. Combine the milk, cocoa powder, and sugar in a small saucepan.
2. Whisk over medium heat until the cocoa and sugar dissolve fully and the mixture is hot.
3. Allow the hot chocolate to cool for 5 minutes.
4. Pour into two mugs and top each with whipped cream and chocolate shavings before serving.

POMEGRANATE SPICE MOCKTAIL

PREPARATION TIME
15 Min

COOL-DOWN TIME
15 Min

SERVINGS
2

Ingredients

- 1 cup (240 mL) pomegranate juice
- 1 cinnamon stick
- 2-star anise
- 1/2 cup (120 mL) sparkling water
- Pomegranate seeds, for garnish

Directions

1. In a small saucepan, pour the pomegranate juice and add the cinnamon stick and star anise.
2. Bring to a simmer for 10 minutes over medium heat. Remove from flame and cool for fifteen minutes.
3. Remove the cinnamon stick and star anise, then divide the liquid between two glasses.
4. Top each glass with sparkling water and garnish with pomegranate seeds before serving.

MAPLE PEAR MOCKTAIL

PREPARATION TIME
5 Min

COOL-DOWN TIME
0 Min

SERVINGS
2

Ingredients

- 1 pear, peeled and cored
- 1 tablespoon (15 mL) maple syrup
- 1 cup (240 mL) sparkling water
- Ice cubes
- Pear slices, for garnish

Directions

1. In a blender, combine the pear and maple syrup. Blend until smooth.
2. Strain the pear mixture into two glasses filled with ice cubes. Top each glass with sparkling water.
3. Stir gently to combine, garnish with pear slices, and serve immediately.

BLUEBERRY BASIL MOCKTAIL

PREPARATION TIME
5 Min

COOL-DOWN TIME
0 Min

SERVINGS
1

Ingredients

- 1/2 cup (120 mL) fresh blueberries
- 5 fresh basil leaves
- 1 tablespoon (15 mL) lemon juice
- 1 tablespoon (15 mL) honey
- 1 cup (240 mL) sparkling water
- Ice cubes

Directions

1. In a glass, muddle the blueberries and basil leaves. Add the lemon juice and honey, then stir to combine.
2. Put ice cubes in the glass and top it off with sparkling water. Stir gently to combine and serve immediately.

MANGO LIME MOCKTAIL

PREPARATION TIME
5 Min

COOL-DOWN TIME
0 Min

SERVINGS
2

Ingredients

- 1 mango, peeled and pitted
- 1 tablespoon (15 mL) lime juice
- 1 cup (240 mL) sparkling water
- Ice cubes
- Mango slice and a lime wheel for garnish

Directions

1. In a blender, combine the mango and lime juice. Blend until smooth.
2. Strain the mango mixture into two glasses filled with ice cubes.
3. Top each glass with sparkling water. Stir gently to combine, garnish with a mango slice and a lime wheel, and serve immediately.

MULLED CRANBERRY MOCKTAIL

PREPARATION TIME
25 Min

COOL-DOWN TIME
10 Min

SERVINGS
4

Ingredients

- 4 cups (960 mL) cranberry juice
- 1 orange, sliced
- 4 whole cloves
- 2 cinnamon sticks

Directions

1. Combine cranberry juice, orange slices, cloves, and cinnamon sticks in a medium-sized saucepan.
2. Take the mixture to a simmer over moderate heat.
3. Let it simmer for 20 minutes to allow the flavors to meld together.
4. Remove from heat and allow it cool for 10 minutes.
5. Strain the mixture to remove solids, pour into glasses, and serve warm.

HONEY LEMON GINGER TEA MOCKTAIL

PREPARATION TIME
25 Min

COOL-DOWN TIME
5 Min

SERVINGS
2

Ingredients

- 2 cups (480 mL) water
- 1-inch piece of fresh ginger, thinly sliced
- 2 tablespoons (30 mL) honey
- 1/4 cup (60 mL) fresh lime juice
- Lemon slices, for garnish

Directions

1. In a small saucepan, combine water and ginger slices. Take to a boil, turn the heat down, and simmer for 15-20 mins.
2. Remove from heat and stir in honey and lemon juice. Let it cool for 5 minutes, then strain it into two mugs.
3. Garnish with lemon slices and serve warm.

SPICED PUMPKIN LATTE MOCKTAIL

PREPARATION TIME
15 Min

COOL-DOWN TIME
5 Min

SERVINGS
2

Ingredients

- 2 cups (480 mL) milk
- 1/4 cup (60 mL) pumpkin puree
- 2 tablespoons (30 mL) sugar
- 1/2 teaspoon pumpkin pie spice
- Whipped cream and extra pumpkin pie spice for garnish

Directions

1. Whisk together milk, pumpkin puree, sugar, and pumpkin pie spice in a small saucepan.
2. Heat over medium heat until hot, but do not boil. Take away from heat and allow it cool for 5 mins.
3. Before serving, pour into two pitchers and garnish with whipped cream and pumpkin pie spice.

PINEAPPLE MINT COOLER

PREPARATION TIME
10 Min

COOL-DOWN TIME
0 Min

SERVINGS
2

Ingredients

- 1 cup (240 mL) pineapple juice
- 1/2 cup (120 mL) soda water
- 10 fresh mint leaves
- Ice cubes
- Pineapple slices and mint sprigs for garnish

Directions

1. Mix the mint leaves at the bottom of your cups. Put ice cubes in the drinks.
2. Pour the pineapple juice over the ice, dividing equally between the two glasses.
3. Top each glass with soda water.
4. Stir gently to combine, garnish with pineapple slices and a sprig of mint, and serve immediately.

RASPBERRY LEMONADE FIZZ

PREPARATION TIME
20 Min

COOL-DOWN TIME
15 Min

SERVINGS
4

Ingredients

- 1 cup (240 mL) fresh raspberries
- 1/2 cup (120 mL) sugar
- 1/2 cup (120 mL) lemon juice
- 2 cups (480 mL) club soda
- Ice cubes
- Raspberries and lemon slices for garnish

Directions

1. In a small non-stick saucepan, mix raspberries, sugar, and lemon juice.
2. Simmer over moderate heat until the sugar dissolves and the raspberries soften.
3. Press the mixture through a fine-mesh sieve into a pitcher, discarding the solids.
4. Allow the raspberry lemonade to cool for 15 minutes. Club soda should be added to the pitcher and mixed in well.
5. Fill four glasses with ice cubes, pour the raspberry lemonade over the ice, and garnish with raspberries and lemon slices before serving.

PEACH ICED TEA MOCKTAIL

PREPARATION TIME
15 Min

COOL-DOWN TIME
15 Min

SERVINGS
4

Ingredients

- 4 cups (960 mL) water
- 4 tea bags
- 1 peach, sliced
- 1/4 cup (60 mL) honey
- Ice cubes
- Peach slices and mint sprigs for garnish

Directions

1. Get some water boiling in a pot.
2. Take it away from heat, add the tea bags, and let steep for 5 minutes. Remove the tea bags, add the peach slices and honey, and stir to combine.
3. Allow the peach iced tea to cool for 15 minutes.
4. Fill four glasses with ice cubes, pour the peach iced tea over the ice, and garnish with peach slices and a sprig of mint before serving.

SHIRLEY TEMPLE

PREPARATION TIME
5 Min

COOL-DOWN TIME
0 Min

SERVINGS
2

Ingredients

- 2 cups (480 mL) ginger ale
- 2 tablespoons (30 mL) grenadine
- 2 maraschino cherries
- Ice cubes

Directions

1. Fill two tall glasses with ice cubes. Pour 1 cup (240 mL) of ginger ale into each glass.
2. Slowly add 1 tablespoon (15 mL) of grenadine to each glass. It should sink to the bottom, then slowly rise, creating a layered effect.
3. Stir gently to mix, if desired.
4. Add a maraschino cherry to each drink and serve right away.

NON-ALCOHOLIC MIMOSA

PREPARATION TIME
5 Min

COOL-DOWN TIME
0 Min

SERVINGS
2

Ingredients

- 1 cup (240 mL) orange juice, chilled
- 1 cup (240 mL) non-alcoholic sparkling wine or grape juice, chilled
- Orange slices for garnish

Directions

1. Pour 1/2 cup (120 mL) of orange juice into the two champagne flutes.
2. Top each flute with 1/2 cup (120 mL) of non-alcoholic sparkling wine or grape juice.
3. Stir gently to combine. Garnish each flute with an orange slice and serve immediately.

VIRGIN APEROL SPRITZ

PREPARATION TIME
5 Min

COOL-DOWN TIME
0 Min

SERVINGS
1

Ingredients

- 1/4 cup (60 mL) non-alcoholic sparkling wine
- 2 tablespoons (30 mL) non-alcoholic bitter aperitif
- A splash of soda water
- Orange slice for garnish

Directions

1. Fill a wine glass with ice. Add the non-alcoholic sparkling wine and the non-alcoholic bitter aperitif into the glass.
2. Add a splash of soda water. Stir gently to mix.
3. Garnish with an orange slice and serve right away.

VIRGIN NEGRONI

PREPARATION TIME
5 Min

COOL-DOWN TIME
0 Min

SERVINGS
1

Ingredients

- 2 tablespoons (30 mL) non-alcoholic gin
- 2 tablespoons (30 mL) non-alcoholic bitter aperitif
- 2 tablespoons (30 mL) non-alcoholic sweet vermouth
- Orange peel, for garnish

Directions

1. Fill a rocks glass with ice. Pour the non-alcoholic gin, non-alcoholic bitter aperitif, and non-alcoholic sweet vermouth into the glass.
2. To combine, stir slowly and carefully. Serve immediately, garnished with the orange peel.

VIRGIN ESPRESSO MARTINI

PREPARATION TIME
5 Min

COOL-DOWN TIME
0 Min

SERVINGS
1

Ingredients

- 1/4 cup (60 mL), espresso, cooled
- 2 tablespoons (30 mL) non-alcoholic coffee liqueur
- 1 tablespoon (15 mL) simple syrup
- Coffee beans, for garnish

Directions

1. Fill a cocktail shaker with ice. Add the cooled espresso, non-alcoholic coffee liqueur, and simple syrup into the shaker.
2. Shake well for about 10 seconds.
3. The mélange is strained into a martini glass. Serve promptly with a few coffee beans as a garnish.

LYCHEE MARTINI

PREPARATION TIME
5 Min

COOL-DOWN TIME
0 Min

SERVINGS
1

Ingredients

- 1/4 cup (60 mL) lychee juice
- 2 tablespoons (30 mL) non-alcoholic vodka
- 1 tablespoon (15 mL) fresh lime juice
- Lychee, for garnish

Directions

1. Fill a cocktail shaker with ice. Add the lychee juice, non-alcoholic vodka, and fresh lime juice into the shaker.
2. Shake well until well combined. Strain the mixture into a martini glass.
3. Garnish with lychee and serve immediately.

VIRGIN FRENCH 75

PREPARATION TIME
5 Min

COOL-DOWN TIME
0 Min

SERVINGS
1

Ingredients

- 2 tablespoons (30 mL) non-alcoholic gin
- 1 tablespoon (15 mL) fresh lemon juice
- 1 tablespoon (15 mL) simple syrup
- 1/4 cup (60 mL) non-alcoholic sparkling wine
- Lemon twist for garnish

Directions

1. Fill a cocktail shaker with ice. Add the non-alcoholic gin, fresh lemon juice, and simple syrup into the shaker.
2. Shake well until well combined. Strain the mixture into a champagne flute.
3. Top with non-alcoholic sparkling wine.
4. Garnish with a lemon twist and serve right away.

VIRGIN DARK AND STORMY

PREPARATION TIME
5 Min

COOL-DOWN TIME
0 Min

SERVINGS
1

Ingredients

- 1/2 cup (120 mL) non-alcoholic ginger beer
- 2 tablespoons (30 mL) fresh lime juice
- 1 tablespoon (15 mL) simple syrup
- Lime wheel and mint sprig for garnish

Directions

1. Fill a highball glass with ice.
2. Add the non-alcoholic ginger beer, fresh lime juice, and simple syrup into the glass.
3. Stir gently to mix. Garnish with a lime wheel & a mint sprig, then serve immediately.

VIRGIN AVIATION

PREPARATION TIME
5 Min

COOL-DOWN TIME
0 Min

SERVINGS
1

Ingredients

- 2 tablespoons (30 mL) non-alcoholic gin
- 1 tablespoon (15 mL) fresh lemon juice
- 2 teaspoons maraschino cherry syrup
- Cherry, for garnish

Directions

1. Fill a cocktail shaker with ice. Add the non-alcoholic gin, fresh lemon juice, and maraschino cherry syrup into the shaker.
2. Shake well until well combined.
3. Strain the mixture into a cocktail glass. Garnish with a cherry and serve immediately.

VIRGIN PISCO SOUR

PREPARATION TIME
5 Min

COOL-DOWN TIME
0 Min

SERVINGS
1

Ingredients

- 2 tablespoons (30 mL) non-alcoholic pisco
- 1 tablespoon (15 mL) fresh lemon juice
- 1 tablespoon (15 mL) simple syrup
- 1 egg white
- Angostura bitters, for garnish

Directions

1. Add the non-alcoholic pisco, fresh lemon juice, simple syrup, & egg white into a cocktail shaker.
2. Shake well until well combined and frothy. Strain the mixture into a rocks glass.
3. Top with a few drops of Angostura bitters and serve immediately.

BLUE LAGOON MOCKTAIL

PREPARATION TIME
5 Min

COOL-DOWN TIME
0 Min

SERVINGS
1

Ingredients

- 1/4 cup (60 mL) blue curaçao syrup
- 2 tablespoons (30 mL) fresh lemon juice
- 1/4 cup (60 mL) lemon soda
- Lemon slice and cherry, for garnish

Directions

1. Fill a highball glass with ice.
2. Add the blue curaçao syrup and lemon juice to the glass. Top with lemon soda.
3. Stir gently to mix. Put a lemon slice and a cherry on top, then serve immediately.

FROZEN PEACH BELLINI

PREPARATION TIME
10 Min

COOL-DOWN TIME
0 Min

SERVINGS
2

Ingredients

- 2 cups (300g) frozen peach slices
- 1 cup (240 mL) non-alcoholic sparkling wine or grape juice
- 2 tablespoons (30 mL) fresh lemon juice
- 1 tablespoon (15 mL) sugar
- Fresh peach slices and mint leaves for garnish

Directions

1. Combine the frozen peach slices, non-alcoholic sparkling wine or grape juice, lemon juice, and sugar in a blender.
2. Blend until smooth.
3. Pour the mixture into two champagne flutes.
4. Serve promptly, garnished with fresh peach slices and mint leaves.

NEW MOTHER MOCKTAIL

PREPARATION TIME
5 Min

COOL-DOWN TIME
0 Min

SERVINGS
1

Ingredients

- 1/2 cup (120 mL) cranberry juice
- 1/2 cup (120 mL) orange juice
- 1/2 cup (120 mL) pineapple juice
- 2 tablespoons (30 mL) grenadine syrup
- Maraschino cherry and orange slice for garnish

Directions

1. Fill a highball glass with ice. Pour the cranberry, orange, and pineapple juice into the glass.
2. Add the grenadine syrup.
3. Stir gently to mix. Add a maraschino cherry and a slice of orange, then serve immediately.

NOPALOMA

PREPARATION TIME
5 Min

COOL-DOWN TIME
0 Min

SERVINGS
1

Ingredients

- 2 ounces (60 mL) fresh squeezed grapefruit juice
- 1 ounce (30 mL) squeezed lime juice
- 3/4 ounce (22 mL) agave nectar
- Salt
- Q Tonic club soda

Directions

1. Combine the grapefruit, lime, and agave nectar in a shaker.
2. Shake well to mix the ingredients. Rim a Collins glass with salt.
3. Fill the glass with ice. Pour the mixture into the glass.
4. Top with Q Tonic Club soda.
5. Stir gently to combine. Serve immediately and enjoy the refreshing Nopaloma!

JASMINE TEA MOCKTAIL

PREPARATION TIME
5 Min

COOL-DOWN TIME
0 Min

SERVINGS
1

Ingredients

- 1/2 cup (120 mL) brewed jasmine tea, cooled
- 1/4 cup (60 mL) pineapple juice
- 1 tablespoon (15 mL) honey
- 1 tablespoon (15 mL) fresh lemon juice
- Fresh mint leaves, for garnish

Directions

1. Combine the brewed jasmine tea, pineapple juice, honey, and fresh lemon juice in a shaker.
2. Shake well to mix the ingredients. Fill a glass with ice.
3. Strain the mixture into the glass. Garnish with fresh mint leaves.
4. Serve immediately and enjoy the refreshing Jasmine Tea Mocktail!

CHOCOLATE FAKE-TINI

PREPARATION TIME
5 Min

COOL-DOWN TIME
0 Min

SERVINGS
1

Ingredients

- 1 ounce (30 mL) chocolate syrup
- 1/2 cup (120 mL) milk
- 1/2 cup (120 mL) cream soda
- Whipped cream, for garnish
- Chocolate shavings for garnish

Directions

1. Drizzle the inside of a martini glass with chocolate syrup. In a shaker, combine the milk and cream soda.
2. Shake well to mix the ingredients. Pour the mixture into the martini glass.
3. Top with whipped cream. Garnish with chocolate shavings.
4. Serve immediately and enjoy the delightful Chocolate Fake-tini!

SNICKERDOODLE COOKIE MOCKTAIL

PREPARATION TIME
5 Min

COOL-DOWN TIME
0 Min

SERVINGS
1

Ingredients

- 1/2 cup (120 mL) milk
- 2 tablespoons (30 mL) vanilla syrup
- 1 tablespoon (15 mL) caramel syrup
- 1/4 teaspoon ground cinnamon
- Crushed Snickerdoodle cookies for rimming
- Cinnamon stick for garnish

Directions

1. Rim the edge of a glass with crushed Snickerdoodle cookies.
2. Combine the milk, vanilla, caramel syrup, and ground cinnamon in a shaker.
3. Shake well to mix the ingredients.
4. Fill the glass with ice. Strain the mixture into the glass.
5. Garnish with a cinnamon stick.
6. Serve immediately and enjoy the delightful Snickerdoodle Cookie Mocktail!

Made in the USA
Coppell, TX
24 November 2023